WHAT TRACK FOR THE ATLANTA FLIGHT?

45 YEARS OF AIRPORT MEMOIRS

JEFF DEGNER

Wasteland Press

www.wastelandpress.net
Shelbyville, KY USA

What Track for The Atlanta Flight?
45 Years of Airport Memoirs
by Jeff Degner

First Printing – October 2020
ISBN: 978-1-68111-379-1

Printed in the U.S.A.

0   1   2   3   4   5   6

TABLE OF CONTENTS

PREFACE

As a customer service agent for Delta Air Lines at Chicago's O'Hare International Airport, my career spanned more than four decades. During this time, I experienced an amazing number of unique, funny, stressful, dangerous, and truly unexpected passenger-related incidents. For years, my family and friends have begged me to put them all down in writing. This book is the result.

INTRODUCTION

Just two months before I graduated from St. Norbert College with a Bachelor of Science degree, both my dad and my mom were understandably curious about just what I planned to do with that degree. Truth be known, I really wasn't sure. So, my mom remarked, "Well, since you enjoy traveling, why don't you consider working for an airline, just for a few years?"

That seemed like a cool idea. Therefore, I drove to O'Hare International Airport the next day and filled out applications with several different major airlines. Delta Air Lines responded promptly and offered to *send me to Atlanta* for a personal interview. Wow. Before long, I was on my way. There I took some tests, had a conversation with the personnel manager and spent the rest of the day sightseeing. Within a week, Delta offered me a job. Thus, in early June of 1970, I began my career in the transportation industry. Later on, I was also offered positions with Eastern and with Braniff. I opted to stick with Delta. That was a good call! Eastern and Braniff no longer exist and Delta was, and still is, a great company to work for.

As I began my airline employment that year, Delta Air Lines still had propeller-driven planes as a part of its fleet. Smoking was allowed anywhere on any flight. In fact, all of the armrests had little metal ashtrays built into them. With few exceptions, there were no advance seat assignments and passengers were simply offered a choice of "window, middle or aisle." By 1973, our customers had a further option of "smoking or non-smoking." It wasn't until 1990 that smoking was completely banned from flights.

Tickets were made of paper and most often were purchased with cash or personal check. Credit cards were seldom used. Classes of service were primarily limited to First Class or Coach, and people tended to dress nicely before flying. Men wore suits and women were in dresses. For many, it was considered a luxury! Types and categories of fares were few and far between, and every passenger had a physical boarding pass, upon which was attached (or printed) their specific seat number. For years, those seats were displayed at the gate on a tab-type seating chart, sometimes visible to the public. Agents soon learned to secretly remove some of the choice tabs from that chart, saving them for VIP customers or unusual requests. There were no frequent flyer programs, no cell phones and no internet!

For the majority of my forty-five years with Delta, I was a gate agent or gate Passenger Service Agent. (PSA) As a PSA, my uniform included a bright red, sport jacket. People with troubling issues were forever looking for the "red coats." I loved working in the hubbub and stress of the gates, and I loved interacting with passengers, colleagues and crew members. The stories you are about to read all deal with some of those interactions, though perhaps, "situations" is the more appropriate word.

In addition to the incidental stories, several Christmastime poems are included. I've written similar poems every December for thirty years, with a variety of themes. However, the poems that are in this book are the only ones related to airports or air travel. Also, interspersed with the memoirs and poems, there are etymological histories, or roots, of many words related to the airline industry. Finally, there is a large section devoted to humor, something that, more than anything else, was a part of every day I worked and for which I became notorious.

Therefore, for those who are about to peruse the following pages, I hope that there will be some learning involved, as well as some thoughtful sighs and maybe a few surprises. Most of all, though, I hope that this book will illicit hearty laughs and some really big smiles.

Now, get ready for takeoff.

JETWAY JETTISON

It was 1971 and early in my airline career. I was working at the ticket counter at when a Latino family came to my attention. The elderly grandmother of the family was flying alone to Miami. It turned out that she spoke only Spanish and needed a wheelchair to get to the departure gate. But her flight was in just thirty minutes! I checked her in, then called for a skycap to quickly take her to her plane. Despite repeated calls, no skycap ever came, so I volunteered to take her myself. On the way, her entire family would be coming with me. Grabbing a wheelchair from a storage room, I helped the grandma into the chair, positioned her feet in the footrests and off we went. Faster and faster I raced down the concourse, leaving various family members trailing behind until only she and I remained. The gate agents knew I was coming and sure enough, as I got to within distant eyesight of the gate, I could see them standing in the hall, pointing to the jetway and shouting, "Hurry! Hurry!" It was now just five minutes till departure time.

Continuing my furious pace, I entered the actual jet bridge and started towards the plane. This is when the disaster occurred. Being a new employee, I didn't know that when you push someone down a jetway in a wheelchair, it is most important to go *backward*. Thus, I never realized what would happen when, *going forward*, the chair would encounter one of the jetway's downward slopes. It was horrible! The footrests of the wheelchair, tipping forward, caught on the floor of the jetway and, since we were still going quite fast, the poor woman was *catapulted* out of the chair, flew through the air and ended up in a heap on the floor. Meanwhile, the flight attendants who were waiting at the door of the aircraft just ahead of us, gasped in disbelief.

What could I say? What could I do? How could I ever explain this to the grandmother's family or my supervisor?

Fortunately, I recalled some of my basic, high-school Spanish and asked, "¿Como está ustéd?" (*how are you*) to which she simply replied, "Bien." (*okay*) Thank God! I helped her to her feet and taking her arm we staggered to the plane together. The flight attendants took over from there. The aircraft still left O'Hare on time and we never heard another word about it. But the image of that grandmother, being jettisoned from that wheelchair, will stay with me forever.

Airplane Etymology 1

Many of the pages in this book include several examples of the etymology or history of airline-related words. Though airplanes today are marvels of the most modern, cutting-edge technology, many of the terms we use today to describe them actually date back hundreds of years and several have interesting origins. All of the examples herein are taken from the Oxford English Dictionary *as well as from online etymological sources.*

An appropriate beginning is the word "plane" itself. Long before the Wright brothers it was understood that when birds were soaring, they held their wings in a rigid, fixed position, i.e. the birds' wings were at a "plane" angle to their bodies. Thus, from the flight of birds came the flight of those things actually constructed with ridged, fixed wings: planes.

THE AUTOGRAPH

At the height of his popularity, Muhammed Ali and his wife, Veronica, were booked to take a Delta flight from O'Hare to Atlanta. I was responsible for that flight and all of us knew, far in advance that this famous man and his spouse would be on board. In the 1990s, Mohammad Ali was one of the most well-known persons on the planet: a three-time world heavyweight boxing champion many consider to be the most charismatic and controversial sports figure of the 20th century. So, I was more than a little excited to learn that I would be working at the departure gate for the flight on which he and Veronica would be passengers.

When Muhammed Ali and Veronica walked down the airport concourse that day, he was greeted by scores of fans and photographers who shouted out, "Ali! Ali!" when, smiling all the way, he passed by. The couple arrived at the gate early and was booked in First Class. To give them an extra bit of privacy, I allowed them to pre-board, several minutes before any other passengers. I realized that I now had a golden opportunity.

I went onboard, carrying a pen and small notebook, and there they were, seated in seats 3A (Muhammed) and 3B (Veronica.) I then said to the great boxer, "Excuse me, Mr. Ali, but could I ask you a favor?"

"Sure," he replied," What can I do for you?"

"I was just wondering if I could have your *wife's* autograph." Muhammed Ali looked like he had just been hit with a powerful right hook.

"What?" he asked, "What? You don't want *mine?*"

I replied, "With all due respect, sir, I figure that thousands of folks have your autograph, but I don't know anyone who has your wife's!"

Turning to Veronica, who was happily signing the notebook, Ali smiled and said to her, "Don't you go giving him your phone number, now!"

I thanked them both, then walked away with the Veronica Ali's autograph. It remains one of my most unusual possessions.

Airplane Etymology 2

"Cockpit" *originated in the 1500's and referred to the pit where fighting cocks did their battle. In other words, it was a small area full of tension and activity. In this sense, the little country of Belgium became known as "the cockpit of Europe" because of all of the battles fought on its soil. It follows, then, that "cockpit" soon became synonymous with the hectic control centers of aircraft, from the earliest biplanes, to war planes, and hence to the airliners of today.*

Inside the cockpit a major control is the "yoke." *Push it forward and the nose drops down. Pull it back and the nose comes up. Thus, our modern yokes help to harness the movement of the airplane much like the yokes of hundreds of years ago helped to harness oxen and other beasts of burden.*

"Steward" *has been in use since the 1400s. Two of the earliest definitions were "master of the ship" and "keeper of the house." Some of today's airline flight attendants (still occasionally called stewards, but not the outdated title, "stewardess,") might argue that those historical meanings can still be quite valid.*

STORY WITH A TWIST

As a new Delta agent, I was asked to provide lunch relief for thirty minutes in the Delta Crown Room, a small but spiffy lounge, away from the hubbub of the terminal. For a membership fee, it provided a nice, quiet place to spend time at the airport, usually before a passenger's departing flight. It also offered complimentary drinks. Many of the commonly asked for alcoholic beverages were typically pre-mixed in convenient little bottles, called "miniatures." So, when the well-dressed businessman approached me at the bar and asked for a vodka martini with a twist, I had no problem at all pouring his drink from the appropriate "Vodka Martini" miniature. Then I spied a bowl of lemon wedges, grabbed one and plunked it into his drink.

"Oh, no!" the man cried. "You've just RUINED the drink, Delta!'

Then, repeating his request, he said, a little louder, "I asked for a martini with a TWIST, not a wedge!"

I was embarrassed about my mixology ignorance. So, I emptied his glass, refilled it with another vodka martini miniature and picked up another lemon wedge. But this time I TWISTED all of the juice out of the wedge, into the glass, just before plopping it into his drink again.

"Arrggghhhh!" the man cried. "You've just ruined *another* drink! Don't you know what a twist is? Arrggghhhh!"

At this point, the kind of twist I was imagining were my hands around his neck. But somehow, I maintained my professional composure. Then I poured him one more drink, this time giving *him* the bowl of wedges. Taking a nearby knife, he went to work on a lemon wedge like an artist, carefully separating all of the pulp from the peel, then, inspecting that skinny, leftover peel, exclaimed, "Now, this is a twist!" Happily, he let it sink into his now-perfect martini and went back into the lounge with a satisfied smile.

This is an old poem that I modernized, first written in the late 1800s by Mary Dow Brine.

SOMEBODY'S MOTHER

The woman was old and ragged and gray
And bent with the chill of the winter's day.
The airport ramp was slick with snow,
And the woman's feet were aged and slow.

She stayed by the terminal and waited long,
Alone, ignored, 'midst the holiday throng
Of hurrying feet that passed her by.
None heeded the plea in her anxious eye.

At last came one of a merry troupe,
The jolliest lad in all the group,
He paused beside her and whispered low,
"I'll help you aboard if you wish to go."

She placed her hand on his strong young arm,
And so, without hesitation or harm,
He guided her unsteady old feet along,
Proud that his own were able and strong.

'Cross the slippery ramp to the airplane they walked.
She held his arm tightly, and smiled as he talked,
To the attendants on board, who took her aside,
And with kindness then said, "In First Class you'll ride!"

Back to his own seat the young man now went,
And spoke to his friends, his heart filled with content.
"She's somebody's mother, for all that we know,
Even though she's aged and ragged and slow."

"And I hope someone else will offer a hand,
To help my mother, you understand.
If ever she's old and trembling and gray,
And her own dear son is far away."

And somebody's mother bent low her head,
As safe at home, much later she said,
"God, be good to the noble boy,
Who is somebody's son and pride and joy!"

STANDBY STRESS

A heartbreaking scene occurred one afternoon as I worked a very crowded flight to Salt Lake City. Even though the flight was overbooked, there were several seats that unexpectedly became available near departure time. This allowed us to accommodate some lucky standbys. Ultimately, there was one seat left, but *two* people, a college-aged couple traveling together still remained on the standby list. Only one could go. There was a tearful goodbye, a last embrace, and then the young man proceeded to slowly walk on board. How sad! Several minutes before departure time, I went down the jetway to dispatch the airplane. Suddenly, a businessman who had been on board ran up to the front of the plane and said he'd just received an emergency call and could no longer take the flight. He had no checked baggage to be removed, and I had just enough time to escort him back to the gate house. The teary-eyed young woman was still there, pensively looking out the window. I yelled over to her, "There's a seat for you! Come quick!"

I've never in my life seen anyone jump so high in delight. Following me back to the plane, I directed her to take the seat that the businessman had just vacated. It was a choice one on the aisle. And…it turned out to be directly next to the middle seat that was *occupied by her astonished boyfriend.* What a fairy-tale ending! I still smile when I think about it.

Airplane Etymology 3

"Ticket" comes from the French word "etiquette," which in turn evolved from the German word, "strechen" which meant, "a little note or notice affixed to something, a label."

LET IT SNOW,
LET IT SNOW,
LET IT SNOW

A significant snowstorm was bearing down on Chicago and O'Hare Airport one wintry afternoon. Flights began to cancel, one by one. It turned out that I would be working the very last flight to Atlanta before the entire airport closed. It was a stressful time, as passengers who were booked on later, cancelled flights, rushed to my gate, hoping to get seats as standbys. Though the original departure time was scheduled to be 1:00 pm, it was delayed until 2:00 pm because of the deteriorating conditions. Eventually, as the runways became snow-covered, that flight became the last Delta departure of the day.

At 2:30 pm, my shift ended, and I left the airport to drive home. Normally, this was an easy, thirty-minute trip. But on this snowy day, the journey lasted almost three hours, with numerous road closures and several accidents. No trip home was ever like it again.

The next day, at 5:00 am, I was on the road once more, ready to go back to work. It was still snowing, though not quite as heavily, and the roads were much easier to navigate.

Ironically, I was once again assigned to work the mornings only scheduled flight to Atlanta. Following the pattern of the day before, all of the previous flights had been cancelled, as well as many in the afternoon. The plane was targeted to leave at 9:00 am. The gatehouse was jammed full of passengers, many of whom had spent a sleepless night in stiff chairs or on cots provided by the airport. However, in addition to all of the folks who were actually *booked* on the flight, there were dozens of displaced customers off of the numerous cancelled flights, all on a huge standby list, praying that a last-minute seat might open up for them.

Unexpectedly, the flight was delayed until 10:00 am. The runways were still ice covered. I made this sad announcement amidst groans and sighs but asked everyone to stay on the concourse just in case there was an update. All Delta announcements could easily be heard on our own concourse. Other concourses and restaurants were farther away, and Delta's announcements competed with those of other airlines.

Unfortunately, at about 9:30AM, the O'Hare control tower said that weather conditions were again deteriorating. Our flight to Atlanta would not be able to leave until noon at the earliest. Oh, no! Once more, there were cries of disbelief and dismay. Once more, I made the bad-news announcement, and yet again asked everyone to stay on the concourse.

Suddenly, at 10:30AM, I received an urgent call from our operations center. There was a brief lull in the storm! I was asked if we could get everyone on board by 11:00AM. I said, "Absolutely!" Within minutes, the flight crew was ready, and boarding began amidst cheers and applause. I made announcements about the new departure time on our own concourse, as well as on the general airport P.A. system. In just fifteen minutes, the gatehouse was empty except for all of the hopeful standby passengers. But there were still twenty open seats on the plane! I knew that these seats belonged to folks who had left the concourse. But now it was too late. Therefore, twenty ecstatic standbys rushed onboard and the plane departed at precisely 11:00AM. Whew!

Then the passengers who had left the concourse started filtering back into the gate, only to learn that their flight had left without them, and that they had just not heard the P.A.s I had made about the sudden, new departure time. I specifically remember that among them was Ted Turner, owner of the Atlanta Braves. Needless to say, there was extreme frustration. But everyone knew that I had warned folks to stay on our own concourse. It was only because they chose not to follow this advice, that others were now residing in their seats. Eventually, the airport reopened, and all the remaining passengers were finally able to depart. And the moral of the story? Listen and heed your gate agents!

MIND THE GAP

As the early-afternoon flight was arriving at the gate in Chicago, I watched the gate agent slowly positioned the ponderous jet bridge into place. Then, standing in the hall, I awaited the deplaning passengers, ready to answer any questions or give directions. Instead, the gate agent himself came rushing out to me. The jetway had stopped but it wasn't quite at the door of the plane! I quickly went to investigate. Sure enough! Though the cabin door was wide open, and I could clearly see all of the passengers lined up in the aisle, ready to leave, I could also see a dangerous, ten-inch gap between the lip of the open airplane door and the leading edge of the jetway. The broken jet bridge simply would not budge, and no amount of button-pushing or power resetting worked. After 15, futile minutes, I made a decision, knowing that there were a hundred arriving passengers anxious to exit the plane. I asked the gate agent to stay at the very end of the jetway to remind and guide every single passenger as they stepped over that gap. I also asked a flight attendant to do the same thing at her end of the door. Finally, I went on board myself and made a careful P.A., informing all of the passengers to use extra caution when stepping out of the plane. With all this in place, I went back into the concourse to meet and greet our relieved customers. It worked like a charm.

When the last passenger had safely deplaned, the flight attendants and pilots also did the same thing. Seeing this, the agent at the end of the jetway also returned to the gate house. Unfortunately, one passenger, a college-aged young woman, was about to leave the plane, when she suddenly realized that she had forgotten her bulky, heavy winter coat. She then returned to her seat in the very rear to remove the coat from the overhead bin. By the time she had bundled the coat in front of her and was carrying it as she walked back to the front, almost all of the flight attendants and pilots didn't realize that *there was still someone on board*. They had already deplaned, and the gate agent had left. Thus, the girl, unattended, stepped off of the plane. Her large winter coat, which she held in front of her, completely obscured her vision of the floor. Did she carefully step over that ten-inch gap and nicely onto the jet bridge? No! Instead, she stepped directly *into* the gap. Her right leg shot into the opening and in the blink of an eye, down she went, directly in front of the last-departing flight attendant who could only look on in horror. I heard the scream from the concourse and raced back down the jetway. Miraculously, the girl was not seriously injured. But her shin was scraped and bleeding, her knee was bruised, and she had huge, ripped holes in the stockings she was wearing, not to mention the dirt and dust from the jetway floor that now coated the bottom of her pretty skirt. She declined any paramedic attention. In fact, she was very anxious to leave, as her new fiancé was waiting for her in the baggage claim area, along with his parents. It was the first time she would see her future in-laws and she had purposely dressed up for the occasion!

Gallantly, I insisted on taking her in a wheelchair myself, apologizing all the way. She insisted that she was all right; I insisted that she let Delta know about the cost to replace any of her damaged garments or any medical fees. Then, I watched her tearful, limping reunion with her future husband while his parents stood with their mouths agape. We never heard another word about it.

Airplane Etymology 4

Since 1750, "galley" has meant a "ships kitchen." But its use goes back even farther than that, all the way to the 1300s, where a galley was a specific type of fast sailing vessel, propelled by oars. The oars were frequently manned by convicts or slaves, and thus to be "work the galleys" was to be punished as a condemned criminal.

HERE SHE COMES!

In the 1980's, I once was an escort for Miss America! Well, actually, she was a *former* Miss America. We knew in advance that she was arriving on a flight into Chicago, then transferring to an American Airlines flight in another terminal. Delta management at O'Hare felt that someone should walk with her to that connecting flight, and I was chosen to be that person. What an honor! This particular Miss America had actually won her crown several years earlier, but that made no difference to me. Therefore, as her arriving flight pulled into the gate, I just couldn't wait to meet her.

She deplaned with a Delta flight attendant who introduced the former pageant winner to me. Miss America was a picture of beauty, charm and poise. I introduced myself, and she smiled, giving me a friendly "Hi." At that moment, though, I couldn't help but notice that she had a *gap* between her front teeth. A gap in Miss America's teeth? I was shocked, but careful not to stare. When I told her that I'd be escorting her over to her American gate, she asked, "You've got my ticket, don't you?

I answered her with a simple, "No."

To which she replied, "Oh crap! This kind of thing happens too often. Crap!"

I was stunned and almost speechless. Miss America used profanity! Somehow, I retained my composure and assured her that, undoubtedly American Airlines already had a ticket waiting for her at her departing gate. She seemed relieved and so off we went, down the concourse. I, Jeff Degner, was escorting Miss America! But then, passing the women's bathroom, she suddenly stopped and said, "I need a cigarette" and stepped inside.

I don't recall too much after that. My mind was still reeling from what I had just witnessed. Miss America was gap-toothed, used bad language and smoked! In looking back at that now, I realize that many of the things I anticipated prior to meeting her came from the way Miss America was viewed back then. Perhaps now outdated, at that time they were the typical, prevailing, chauvinistic notions of what this "ideal" woman would be like. In fact, Miss America could have been any of the women stepping off of that plane.

Airplane Etymology 5

Many aircraft terms have colorful nautical origins. Planes are commonly called "ships" and like ships, are always referred to as feminine in gender. (For example, "she's a little tail-heavy, but she'll fly!") "rudder" is another example. No plane nor ship is without one. When you entered an airliner today, you "boarded" the flight. This particular use of the verb "board" began in the 1500s. The ships at that time were all made of wood, (boards) and to approach the sides of these ships, or to enter a vessel, was to go "aboard." Similarly, "starboard" also referred to the right side of a ship, while the left side was "larboard" (now an uncommon word, replaced instead with "port.") By the way, though this has never been proven, many folks believe that the word "posh" was originally an acronym for where the best cabins were located in the ocean liners sailing to and from America, i.e. "Port Over, Starboard Home" as these rooms avoided the direct glare and heat of the sun. The word bulki meant "cargo" in Old Norse. Sometime in the 15th-century sailors and builders in Europe realized that walls within a vessel would prevent cargo from shifting during passage. So, walls that were installed abeam (side-to-side) in a vessel's hull were called "bulkheads."

NATHAN'S UPGRADE

*(I wrote this in 2002. It appeared in the book,
"Chicken Soup for the Traveler's Soul")*

At my desk at O'Hare one day, this phone call came through.

"Mr. Degner," he began, "you probably don't remember meeting me and my family back in November. We were going to Orlando and the flight was overbooked."

I confessed that I couldn't recall the occasion.

"You made an announcement asking for volunteers willing to give up their seats for free tickets and a later flight. My wife went up to your desk and told you that all four of us, myself, my wife, our daughter Mariah, and our son Nathan, would be willing to go later."

The story still didn't ring a bell.

"Well," he went on, "we gave you our tickets but about twenty minutes later, you came back and said that you wouldn't need our seats after all."

At this point I still was unsure just where my former customer was going with his phone call. Was he angry that his family didn't get their free tickets?

The man continued, "So you gave our tickets back and then you told us that you had "upgraded' our seats to First Class as a way of way of showing gratitude for our willingness to be bumped. Now, I know that this was something you didn't have to do--you could have just as easily left us with our original coach seats. Now do you remember us?"

"Yes, I think I do recall meeting you." I still wasn't *sure* I was recollecting the same family, but, as he seemed pleased and not upset about something I had done, my biggest reaction was a sense of relief. "I'm glad you enjoyed those seats so much," I said.

"Oh, we did! That flight to Orlando was wonderful," he replied. My wife and I sat next to each other and we even got champagne before takeoff. Mariah and Nate were directly across from us, and we laughed and talked all the way to Florida. It was just fantastic."

"I'm really glad that you and your family were happy with the seats, and I thank you for taking the time to call--"

"There's something more," he said. I noticed a sudden shift in the tone of his voice.

"A few days after we got home from our vacation..." I could sense an awful pain in his voice as he continued, "Nathan was out riding his bike and..." he hesitated, "the driver of the car didn't even see him..."

He couldn't finish his sentence, but I knew what had happened. My eyes welled up as I waited in silence.

A moment later, the boy's father went on, "That trip was the last week the four of us were together. We'll always remember that flight to Orlando, all of us sitting in those First-Class seats. We were so happy, and Nathan had so much fun. It meant so much to him. You helped make that time special,

Mr. Degner. My wife and I just wanted to say how much we appreciate the gift you gave us."

I was speechless. I breathed in deeply and, somehow, I found the words to express my sympathy for his terrible loss and thanked him for sharing his story with me.

After we said goodbye, I sat down and cried for this little boy and his grieving family. I hadn't realized how much their upgrade had meant to them on their final trip with their son. It was, after all, just a routine procedure and something that I gave little thought to.

A few months later, Nathan's father visited me at the airport. He and his wife and daughter were taking their first flight since the accident. I shook his hand warmly and thanked him once again for the phone call. He, in turn, gave me a small photograph of Nathan.

It has now been many years since that brief visit, but Nathan's picture has been with me ever since. I keep it as a monument to a boy who is no longer with us, and a constant reminder that we never know when even the smallest gesture can touch others in an unexpected and extraordinary way.

POEM 2 (1990)

The airport during Christmas time displays a certain glow
As passengers with packages go hustling to and fro,
And moms and dads and tiny tots just seem to smile more
While they board their gleaming airplanes
and pass that jetway door.

The colors green and red embellish all the concourse shops,
And janitors sing "Jingle Bells" while plying brooms and mops.
The twinkling lights of aircrafts mimic those on Christmas trees,
And travelers in the chapel give their thanks on bended knees.

Those of us who work these flights relive some common scenes
And find that Santa Claus is never absent from our dreams.
Flight Attendants sometimes seem like busy little elves
As they dip inside their galley carts pulling things from shelves.

And pilots lead their shiny jets like reindeer with their sleigh,
Some even saying "ho ho ho" to shock the F.A.A.!
Agents check their standby lists for all good girls and guys
And try their best to give first class to each V.I.P. who flies!

But as for me, my poetry is meant to make you smile.
I hope it helps the Christmas glow stay with you for a while.
With love and peace and happiness and lots of daily cheer,
I wish you all the very best in a promising new year.

ABOUT FACE

Just fifteen minutes before the fully booked Delta flight was to leave for Atlanta, a First- Class passenger rushed up to the boarding gate. She was a businesswoman, dressed impeccably, with her hair, nails, and makeup done in flawless style. She also appeared to be really angry, muttering something about "long security lines," then stomping onto the aircraft to take her pre-reserved and coveted, bulkhead-aisle seat.

There were just a few other passengers who boarded in the next couple of minutes: a family with a crying baby, two lovers, arm-in-arm, a G.I. returning from leave, and some last-minute standbys.

I was the gate agent responsible for the flight. As I put the final paperwork onboard and prepared to dispatch the plane, I glanced at that First-Class bulkhead aisle seat to see if our angry passenger had regained her composure.

She was gone! Instead, the G.I. was sitting in that coveted spot, now with a big grin on his face. Our irritated prima donna had given him her seat. She, with her fancy clothes and perfect appearance, was now occupying a middle seat in the back of the plane. Somehow, I know that she must have been smiling too.

CASE HISTORY

Years ago, and before Transportation Security Administration (TSA) began, passengers on a Delta flight sometimes had delicate items to check which needed to be claimed immediately upon arrival, before even making their way to the baggage claim area. These items included things like wheelchairs and strollers, or fragile items like paintings or guitars, all of which were "gate tagged." Ramp personnel then quickly brought them up into the jetway, often before regular baggage was unloaded from the bins.

On one rainy evening, a man was waiting for his piece of gate-tagged luggage: An expensive classical guitar in a costly case. After too much time had gone by, he approached me and asked if there was a problem. I called the ramp via radio but got no answer, so I opted to go out onto the tarmac, despite the rain, and look for it myself. He watched out of the window.

Walking on the ramp, past and over pieces of the usual airplane loading equipment, I made my way to the first bin of the plane. There it was! The ramp agent had set it aside, but then somehow forgot what he'd done. Feeling happy that I had found it, I grabbed it securely in both hands and started hurrying back to the gate.

This is when an unfortunate circumstance occurred. The airplane was attached to a tug by a steel tow bar. I needed to cross over that bar to get back to the gate. But I *tripped* over it instead, and soon found myself flying face first towards the wet and dirty ramp. It would have been a bad tumble, but, since I still had the guitar case in both hands, I used it like a shield, keeping it under my chest as I fell. I distinctly remember the sound and feel of the *scraping* of tiny bits of debris from the ground, imbedding themselves into the case. How embarrassing! Fortunately, none of my Delta ramp colleagues had witnessed my gyrations. Even more fortunately, I was not injured, and my uniform was unmarked.

Not so with the poor case. I picked myself up and slowly brought it back into the gate house, then put it, scratched, dirty and dented, into the horrified hands of the owner. Fortunately, the guitar itself, nestled inside, was fine. The distressed passenger spent a long time in our baggage service office filling out a damaged bag report. Among all of my airline experiences, this "case" was surely the most unique.

Airplane Etymology 6

"Tarmac" is commonly referred to as the paved part of an airport where planes stop to take on or let off passengers. In the early 1800s, a Scottish engineer named John Loudon McAdam developed a technique of road construction using layers of small pieces of stone. The resultant surface was referred to as "macadam" and this layering process still exists in many roads today. In the early 20th century, an English surveyor named Hooley developed a technique for combining tar with macadam to produce a newer road-building material. It was called tar macadam and abbreviated to "tarmac." Although tarmac was used extensively in the construction of airports during World War II, no major airport now uses it. The pavement at major airports is now usually asphalt or concrete.

MEMORABLE MOMENTS

An elderly lady slowly approached me one day and said, "What track for the Atlanta flight?" I told her "Track E6" and off she went with a smile.

Over the airport public address system. came the announcement, "Mr. Tom Brinkman, please report to gate twelve immediately, your aircraft is preparing for departure." At that exact moment, a man raced past me and I assumed it was Tom Brinkman. He paused only to *scream* a reply to the P.A. speaker in the ceiling of the concourse, 'I'm just running past gate four! Wait!"

One morning, a worried-looking young man came up to me at the counter and said, "I'm looking for arriving flight 2105, and I can't find it. My new girlfriend, Mary Margaret, is on it along with her parents, and I told them I'd be waiting for them at their arrival gate. It's now 10:30, and the flight was supposed to come in at 10:20. Help!"

I immediately looked up Ms. Margaret's name on flight 2105 in the computer. Sure enough, there it was, right on time. And it had recently landed, correctly, at *Midway Airport.* I won't repeat the terrible words he used just then, but he took off running towards the taxi stand. Midway was at least 45 minutes away. I wondered if their relationship was about to have its first major challenge.

During a chaotic shift amidst a summer storm, a passenger slowly walked up to me and asked, "Where is the X concourse?" I said, "X?"

"Yes!" he replied, "I know that this is the L concourse, but when I looked up the gate for my flight, it said, "**XLD**." Where is that gate?" (*In airline jargon: XLD means "cancelled" Uh-oh.*)

A customer asked me to make sure his new, frequent-flyer number was in his record. He went by the name of "Rick Jensen," but "Rick" was actually his *middle* name, and that's the one he preferred to use. The name on all of his legal documents was "P. Rick Jensen." After he presented his new, frequent flyer card to me, I suggested that he might want to get a replacement. I am unable to write this indelicate word, but, his first initial on that card, as well as his middle name, had been *combined*, without any period or space. Hmmm!

Completely unattended, a small boy came up to my desk one day and said, "My mom is lost! Can you find her?" I asked him his name, and he said, "Danny Whitney." So, over the airport P.A. I paged to my gatehouse, "The mother of little Danny Whitney." Within seconds, a very distraught woman raced into the gate, saw Danny and swooped him up into her arms. Somehow, they had gotten separated on the concourse. It may have been the best reunion I ever saw.

POEM 3 (1994)

At Christmastime, the earth was kissed,
By nature with a gloss of white.
And even through the evening mist,
Could oft be seen a twinkling light,
Upon the wings of jets that hissed,
Like streaks, they flashed across the night.

Inside these soaring ships of steel,
Rode festive folks from far-flung states.
Attendants offered each a meal,
While pilots flew at speedy rates.
And happiness did each one feel:
They parked on time at all their gates.

These Yuletide special airline scenes,
Can have a heartfelt happy glow.
Amidst the hues of reds and greens,
As travelers rush to those they know.
For Peace and Love this season means.
Merry Christmas! Ho, ho, ho!

LOSING HIS SHIRT

One day, acting as a red-coated Delta PSA, I was asked to meet
an inbound flight from Ohio. On it was a Mr. James Walters.
En route to Chicago, a flight attendant had spilled Coke all
over his nice, white shirt. The flight attendant would be
escorting Mr. Walters off the plane to see what we could do
about it, if anything, at O'Hare.

Mr. Walters and flight attendant Kathy soon found
themselves in front of me in the concourse. The stain on
Walter's shirt was horrible. However, it was located low
enough on his shirt that I felt that his sport jacket, if buttoned,
would cover it nicely. I apologized profusely and suggested this
as a *temporary* remedy, adding that Delta would certainly pay
for his shirt to be cleaned at his convenience. Unfortunately,
he didn't have a sport jacket. He was in town for just a few
hours to be interviewed for a management job.

Then I recalled that O'Hare had a store where men's shirts
were sold. I asked Walters his shirt size and then arranged to
have another agent purchase a new, white shirt for him. Mr.
Walters, Kathy and I all waited several minutes for it to be
delivered by the hustling agent. As the new shirt, still in its
pristine packaging, arrived at the gate, Mr. Walters was really
happy. He turned to Kathy and me, said, "Thank you so

much!" and immediately went into the men's bathroom to put it on.

A few minutes later he came out with a big smile on his face. "How do I look?" he said. "It fits perfectly!" Kathy and I assured him that it looked just wonderful. With that, a beaming James Walters practically pranced down the hall on his way at last to his big interview.

That's when Kathy turned to me and said, "It looked like *shit* on him!" In fact, Kathy was right. The shirt, being brand new and just out of the package, had very noticeable creases where it had originally been factory-folded. Most likely, it had also been on the shelf for weeks. Furthermore, I had forgotten the fact that this airport store catered primarily to *airline employees*. As Mr. Walters happily walked away, we both noticed that on each shoulder were large, pilot-type *epaulets*. Hope his interview was more of a good fit.

HIGH FIVES

I was assigned to work a fully booked flight one morning. I had only one partner. She was a competent agent and we worked well together. The inbound plane came in late, thus, we had minimum time in which to get the outbound flight out, while still maintaining the all-important, on-time departure.

As check in proceeded, together we handled the usual hectic tasks. There were folks in wheelchairs who needed to be preboarded and dozens of anxious standby passengers. There was a "Gold Medallion" flyer (upper echelon of frequent flyers) who wanted us to get him out of his middle seat. There was a family of five who wanted seats together, and at least one passenger who spoke Spanish only. In addition, a few customers were hoping for an upgrade, and at least a dozen customers whose bags needed to be gate-checked.

We also had to start and end the boarding process, keep accurate count of all the people on board, deliver important paperwork to the pilots and flight attendants and finally get the flight out, right on schedule.

What a whirlwind it was! After the wheelchairs, preboards, standbys, upgrades, family-of-five and Spanish speaker were all nicely accommodated, we raced down the jetway, paperwork in hand, all in perfect order. We closed the door of the plane, withdrew the jetway, saw the plane pushing out on time, walked back to the gate house and, (I remember this clearly) gave each other a happy and relieved high-five, knowing that we'd done a good job.

That's when the Gold Medallion flyer came up to us and said, "Well, were you able to get me out of that middle seat?" Oh, no! Somehow in all the turmoil, we both had completely forgotten his simple request.

Miraculously, we were able to arrange for our forgotten passenger to have a nice first-class seat on the very next flight. Furthermore, rather than being furious, he actually was rather bemused at what had happened. Ruefully, my partner and I recalled that high five we had just given each other so enthusiastically. Even years later, we still laughed about it.

Airplane Etymology 7

Next to the tail in an airplane are devices called elevators. An "elevator" is a primary flight control surface that controls movement about the lateral axis of the plane. This movement is referred to as "pitch." Most aircraft have two elevators. The origin of "elevator" began in the 1600's and is derived from the Latin word, elevare, *which referred to a human muscle specifically used for raising. You might have ridden in an elevator to rise to the concourse level of an airport. The definition of "pitch" goes back even farther to the 1200s and Old English, where it was derived from* picche, *meaning "thrust downward towards the ground." Today's baseball and cricket players, as well as opera singers, also use this common word.*

MIX MASTER

Almost 20 years after my one, brief experience as a bartender in the Delta Crown Room, I was assigned to work there again for just a thirty-minute, lunchtime relief. I assumed that I'd be at the "meet and greet" front desk area. But no, I was to stand in for the regular bar tender once more. I was now twenty years wiser and a bit more experienced in mixology. However, the Crown Room had grown immensely in size and now offered a much greater variety of beverages than ever before. Saying that, though, I still felt pretty relaxed and confident as various members approached the bar. Easily, I dispensed cold beer right out of the tap and poured it into frosted mugs. Red wine? No problem. Coke? Seven-Up? Pre-mixed martinis? Piece of cake, even adding the proper twists as I had learned so many years ago.

Then the red wine drinker came back with a frown, and I could see that his glass was only half full. "Delta," he said, "This is terrible wine. It tastes awful!" I apologized, grabbed a brand-new bottle and poured him another glassful. He stopped, sniffed, took a tiny sip, swirled it around his mouth and then said, "Much better!" and left with a contented smile. Whew!

One of the very next customers asked for what sounded like "Canvas Stir."

"I'm sorry," I said, "but, could you tell me again what beverage you wanted?"

He repeated, more slowly "Courvoisier."

I was totally perplexed. What was that? I had no idea. Frantically, I scanned all of the bottles that were on hand until I spotted the one with "Courvoisier" on the label. Whew. Grabbing a large tumbler, I competently added some ice, then carefully poured enough of the beverage to fill it to the top.

The passenger seemed unusually delighted, and said, "Wow! Thanks, Delta!"

When Bob, the regular bartender came back, he noticed the bottle of Courvoisier had been seriously depleted. "Degner" he said, "What happened to all the Courvoisier?"

I explained how happy the Crown Room member had been with what I had given him.

Only then did I learn that this beverage is a very expensive liqueur and is only served in very small quantities. No wonder the customer was so happy.

Then I pointed out the bad bottle of red wine. Bob looked aghast, and asked me, how much of the wine did this dissatisfied customer actually swallow?

"Half a glass."

Bob then pointed out that the first bottle of red wine that I had served the man from was a *display bottle.* It was not full of red wine, but rather water, tea and colored dye, all to make it look like a real bottle while it sat out on the display shelf, hour after hour, day after day.

For some reason, I was never asked to work in the Crown Room again.

Airplane Etymology 8

During the time of Columbus, sailing ships kept track of their speed by means of a thin quadrant of wood with was loaded so as to float upright. It was known as a "log" and was connected to a length of line, then wound around a reel which played out as the ship moved. The record distance traveled was kept in a little ledger near the reel called a "log book." Every airliner has one today.

POEM 4 (1997)

Miles above the city streets, miles above the eaves,
The planes flash by, in the sky, like Flying Christmas Trees.
With lights that twinkle green and red, they seem to send a code,
Bringing warmth and smiles even when the days are cold.
"Peace on Earth, goodwill to all", this message in the sky
Is signaled by the lights upon the planes as they go by.

On the ground these Flying Trees are tended to by elves,
Who do their jobs in well-trained teams,
or sometimes by themselves.
They get each Tree all ready for its next departing flight
And clean those twinkling lights
that are seen throughout the night.
Other elves will stay on board to tend to every rider,
Serving food and beverages like wine or apple cider.

The Flying Christmas Trees arrive at lots of different stations,
Taking all their passengers to many different nations.
Santa's helpers fly each Tree with rarely a delay,
While keeping watch on radar for eight reindeer and a sleigh.
From Nome to Nicaragua and from Bombay to Belize,
The message that they echo is heard best on Christmas Eve.

You see, elves and Santa's helpers and lights of red and green
Are components of the magic inside every yuletide scene.
And this magic that they symbolize, this wonder and this joy,
Is felt inside the open hearts of every girl and boy.
A worthy goal, it could be said, in December or in May,
Would be to feel this happy glow on each and every day.

And so, my friends, I write this poem and hope it makes you smile,
And nestles in your heart and makes you happy for a while.
I wish you Merry Christmas and Happy New Year, too,
May the wonder of the twinkling lights be felt in all of you,
Whether you are home, or in a church on bended knees,
Or high up in the sky inside those Flying Christmas Trees

UPWARD SOLDIER

As a gate agent working a busy, late-December flight to Atlanta, I was approached by a young woman who asked me if there were any First-Class seats available. She wanted to buy *two*, despite any cost, for a pair of uniformed soldiers she had seen together in the gate. Furthermore, she wanted to do so completely anonymously. She only said, "I think I'm going to a much happier place than they are."

As it turned out, the First-Class cabin was full, and there was a waiting list of thirty business-elite passengers hoping that someone might not show up in time for one of those highly coveted seats. So, this kind lady then volunteered to simply trade her own First-Class seat for the coach seat held by one of the soldiers. She had spotted the name "Clark" on a duffel bag that was laying by their feet in the gate house. I thanked her warmly for her compassion and made the appropriate seat-switches in the computer. She was now in coach, and a fortunate soldier named Clark was now in First-Class. As the flight began to board, I paged Mr. Clark up to the desk.

Both G.I.s immediately came forward. I told them that one of them, just by the luck of the draw, had been upgraded by a passenger who wanted to remain anonymous. I then gave the First-Class seat to young Mr. Clark. He looked at it and beamed! His partner also looked at it with a big smile. It was then that Mr. Clark said to his fellow soldier, "I want you to have it." Thus, on that flight to Atlanta, there were three passengers with happier hearts. One was the generous woman who first gave up her choice, First-Class seat. One was Mr. Clark, who then unselfishly gave away that same seat to his friend. And one was the absolutely delighted soldier who was now sitting up front. I felt privileged to have witnessed this, and I became the fourth person with a happier heart. What a reflection of the true meaning of Christmas.

A SHORT STORY

I met Karl Slover, one of the longest-surviving, original, "Munchkins" in the *Wizard of OZ* movie as he was flying out of O'Hare to a Munchkin reunion in Atlanta. We had a great conversation about his dual roles in that famous, old movie. Not only was he cast as one of the townspeople in *OZ*, but he was also proud to have played the First Trumpeter.

Several years later, I saw him again on a flight I was working. His health had deteriorated, however, and he was now confined to a wheelchair. Since he recognized me, I offered to take him down the jetway myself, rather than using a skycap.

Parking the wheelchair at the end of the jetway, I stepped in front of the chair and greeted the waiting flight attendants. As I was doing so, another agent came up to the back of Stover's chair with some paperwork for the pilots. Without looking, I simply reached back to take those pre-flight documents. But at that exact moment, Mr. Slover decided to *stand up*, rather than remaining seated. Thus, when I reached back, I ended up smacking him right in his little, wrinkled nose. Tears came to his eyes, but he said he was fine, fine and he hobbled on board.

Ever since then, though, I became known as the guy who punched the munchkin.

GOODY! TWO SHOES!

As a gate agent, my job was to always make sure flights were handled smoothly and safely and, of course, that they all departed on time. One day a flight attendant from a plane which was about to leave for Tampa came running out to advise me that an elderly passenger had left her "orthopedic shoes" at the security checkpoint and was quite upset about it. Apparently, she had worn dressier shoes while in the airport. Her walking shoes were the ones left behind, and it was these which she used in the regular, daily activities of her life.

It was just four minutes to departure time and the concourse security point was far away. Our elderly passenger couldn't possibly go back to get the shoes herself. In addition, it was the last direct flight of the day to Tampa, so sending them to her later wasn't a good option. I turned over the gate operation to my colleagues and set off at a brisk jog to the distant checkpoint. I also grabbed a radio to keep in touch with the gate agents and with the crew on board. Though the concourse was crowded, folks could see me racing along and quickly moved aside.

Sure enough, the shoes, which were tucked inside a green shopping bag, were neatly set aside by the security personnel, waiting for someone to come back for them. However, by the time I arrived, huffing and puffing, and then hustled back to the departure lounge, the flight had already been pushed out of the gate by a ramp tug. Using the radio, though, I communicated with the captain, told him what was going on, and asked him to watch out his window for me.

I hustled down the gatehouse stairs and out onto the inner taxi way until I was directly beneath the large 767. As I approached, the pilot opened the cockpit window and looked down at me, shaking his head in disbelief. I planned to effortlessly toss the shoes up to him, but I quickly realized that it would be somewhat more challenging than I had imagined. In addition to the noise and commotion on the tarmac at that moment, the distance from where I stood on the ground to where the pilot was in the window seemed vast, almost three stories up. Furthermore, the cockpit window slanted in, thus the throw would have to be kind of a high loop. Finally, the motion needed to be a soft underhand, rather than an overhand fling: challenging but do-able.

Taking one shoe out of the green bag, I confidently tossed it up towards the window. But the throw was embarrassingly short, and the shoe fell back down to the ramp with a thud. My second throw perfectly arced its way just to the *left* of my target. All of my skills at pitching a softball had suddenly abandoned me. However, my third try saw that orthopedic shoe softly sail straight into the captain's waiting arms. Hurray! By this time, the ramp tug had now been disconnected, all the loading equipment had moved away, and the airplane had been given permission from the control tower to depart. Several ramp employees working nearby flights incredulously watched what was going on and must have thought I had lost my mind.

Meanwhile the second shoe patiently waited for the reunion with its sole mate. It would not have to wait long. Though my final toss seemed much too high, somehow, the pilot reached way out and snagged it with one hand. Even Jerry Rice couldn't have made a better touchdown catch. The captain gave me a triumphant thumbs-up and a huge grin which matched the one on my own face.

When I returned to the gatehouse, the people who were there broke into cheers and applause. I don't think that our elderly passenger ever realized the efforts that led to the retrieval of her two orthopedic shoes, but she probably is still wondering what happened to that green shopping bag. As for me, I still smile every time I think about it. And every once in a while on the softball field, I practice tossing a shoe just in case.

POEM 5 (1999)

Oh my gosh, it's here already: Christmastime anew,
With its special glow a part of everything we do.
Travelers for the holidays are hustling down the halls,
While harried Delta PSAs make their final calls.

Flight attendants try to stow all those coats and cases,
Somehow keeping charming smiles etched upon their faces.
Pilots hope they won't be held by A.T.C. delays,
And yuletide songs are often heard on terminal P.A.s

There's a feeling in this air that comes just once a year.
It's in the hearts of those who still think about reindeer.
And in the eyes of tiny tots who sit on Santa's lap,
And even in our dreams as we take our winter's nap.

I know not what this feeling's called, this special Christmas joy
That makes us recollect our years as tender girl or boy,
But somehow in December, not summer, spring or fall,
We really tend to think about the words, "Goodwill to all"

This is what I wish for you, wherever you may be:
May your home have lots of glow, beyond the Christmas tree.
And may your hearts be happy and your flights all land on time,
And may you find much comfort with songs like *Auld Lang Syne.*

REAL CELEBRITIES

As public-contact, airline employees, we always had briefings before we started our shift. These were just little meetings that let us know about any unusual, important or sensitive issues that might be ahead of us that day. In one such briefing, the supervisor on duty said that later in our shift, a major television studio would be filming a <u>national commercial</u>. It would take place on our concourse, and at one of our gates! This commercial would feature Delta Air Lines and Delta's new flight schedule to Orlando. The supervisor said, "We need someone to act the role of a gate agent meeting and greeting two celebrities, prior to them boarding their Delta flight."

The room grew silent. Then, for some mysterious reason, the supervisor turned to me and said, "Jeff, would you be interested?"

Of course, I was *more* than interested. Already I was thinking, "O'Hare today, Hollywood tomorrow." My new acting career was surely going to get off to a good start.

A few hours later, I was at one of our gates being fitted for a tiny, lapel mike and undergoing some sound and lighting checks with the WGN-TV technicians. "Relax!" they said. "Just act normally, speak normally, and greet the celebrities like you'd greet any passenger"

I asked who the two celebrities were.

"They're currently waiting for their cue in the Delta Crown Room."

I was getting more and more excited, just trying to imagine who they might be. Movie stars? Well-known Chicago athletes? Politicians?

Finally, all preparations were done, and I received the word that the two celebrities were already walking down the concourse and would enter the gate in moments. Extra stage lights went on, there was total silence, and I prepared myself to deliver my usual, normal greeting to whomever these famous people might be.

At that precise moment, two clowns walked up to me! They were "Bozo" and "Cookie," supposedly about to take a "Delta Dream Vacation" to Orlando." The cameras rolled, and I somehow was able to hide my dismay at not meeting a superstar. I greeted Bozo and Cookie just like any other passenger. Later, they posed for pictures with me. In viewing the pictures, my Delta colleagues invariably said, "Wow! Look at the three clowns!"

For the record, an actual commercial was made by WGN that day, and it was on the air, all across the United States, for months. My brief part was only about 20 seconds long. I never did pursue a Hollywood acting career after that. However, a video of what would have surely been my Oscar-winning performance is still visible on YouTube via this hyperlink.

Copy and paste
https://www.youtube.com/watch?v=6_8ksBO6Pg
Or do a YouTube search under "Bozo Jeff"

Just try not to laugh at the three clowns!

LANGUAGE ARTS

I speak passable Spanish and all of my Delta colleagues knew this. One day they brought over an elderly lady whom, they said, only spoke Spanish, and asked me to tell her that her flight was delayed, but that she'd still have time to make her connecting flight. This I did, confident in my almost bi-lingual ability. Sadly, she didn't understand me. So, using much simpler language and speaking a bit louder, I repeated, again in my near-perfect Spanish, "Your. Flight. Is. Delayed." Unfortunately, she still looked confused! Noticing that she was clutching her ticket and passport, I held out my hand for both. After looking at her passport, I soon saw that she was from *Bulgaria*. No wonder she didn't understand a word I said.

One of my most memorable Spanish-speaking experiences was when I was asked to speak, *in Spanish*, to a deranged-looking man, who said he had a bomb strapped to his back. A bomb! In my basic, high school Spanish class, we never learned how to translate the word "bomb." So, with our own English word in my mind, I converted it into something that *might* have been Spanish and asked him if he was carrying a "*bomba.*" He looked disgusted, shook his head no, and then something like "*Gringo estupido*" before the police took him away. As it turns out, "bomba" is the exact Spanish translation for bomb or any type of explosive device. I truly didn't know this at the time. I will never forget it now.

On another occasion, a swarthy man wearing a cowboy hat approached my desk and seemed to be a little confused. He presented his boarding pass and on it I could clearly see the name, "Francisco Sanchez."

I immediately spoke to him in his native tongue and confidently told him, in my near-perfect Spanish, that his flight was on time and that it would begin boarding in ten minutes.

He looked at me, then said with a pronounced Texas drawl, "I don't have the slightest idea what you just said!"

I was astonished. And embarrassed, too. I asked him how it was possible, with a name like Francisco Sanchez, that he didn't understand Spanish? He went on to tell me that his grandparents were from Mexico, but his parents were born in Dallas. He, too, was born in Texas, but he absolutely refused to learn any Spanish, considering English to be his only, native tongue. In college, when learning a second language was a requirement, he took German.

One morning a young man timidly approached my position at the Delta ticket counter and, pointing to himself, said, "No English." I acknowledged him with a nod and a welcoming smile.

Then he said what sounded like, "Blue flu?" in a questioning way.

I asked, "Blue flu?" and shook my head slightly, indicating that I didn't understand him. He tried again, "Boo flu?"

I once more expressed confusion.

He tried yet again, as I listened closely, "Boo faloo?"

Hard as I tried to guess his intention, whatever he was attempting to say just wasn't sinking in.

Finally, out of verbal options, he removed a map of the United States from his back pocket, and, pointing to the state of New York, placed his finger directly over the city of *Buffalo*. He was asking about flights to Buffalo! Unfortunately, Delta did not fly out of O'Hare to that city, so I simply directed him over to the nearby American Airlines area. There, I imagine, he already had his map out.

CAST CALL

The well-dressed passenger came to our gate in a wheelchair. He was huge, perhaps six-feet-five, and looked to be at least 300 pounds. Wearing a fitted sport jacket and slacks, this former NFL player had recently suffered a compound fracture of his left leg. Now the leg was in a complete, solid cast from his ankle to his thigh, sticking out in front of the wheelchair like a battering ram. He could stand on his right leg but could not walk. As an early-boarder, my gate house partner and I opted to take him to the front of the plane in his wheelchair then, since it was much too wide to fit down the airplane's aisle, we would transfer him to a much narrower wheelchair, called a "straight back" which the airlines used just for this purpose. My partner was a big guy himself, so I anticipated that there would be no problems.

The transfer to the straight back occurred quite smoothly. The plan I then suggested was to roll the former football player down the inside of the cabin *backwards*, until he was directly next to his row of seats. After that, he would be able to get himself up and into his assigned place. Thus, my partner pulled the straight back from behind, slowly walking backwards, while I pushed from the front. It was hard work! Fortunately, the targeted seats were near the front of the coach cabin.

Suddenly the chair hit a seam in the carpet of the plane which completely stopped our motion. I spoke with my partner and said, "Okay, on the count of three, pull very firmly and I'll push hard."

Just as I anticipated, the straight back hesitated...then lurched backwards on its way. But at that exact time a terrible and loud *ripping* sound occurred. As it turned out, the straight back had not hung up on a seam in the carpet. Rather, the passenger's sport jacket had flopped open and somehow the lower, inside pocket hooked itself on an armrest we had passed. This, alone, was what had stopped our initial momentum. The ripping sound was the sound of that inner pocket, along with a quantity of lining, literally tearing away from his nice jacket!

For a moment, time seemed to stand still. The look of shock on our passenger's face was minor compared to the looks of horror on ours. Immediately afterwards, he *could* have been pretty upset, maybe even furious. But he just calmly accepted what had happened without saying a word. All we could do was apologize profusely and direct him to the baggage service office at his destination where he could fill out an official "damaged/destroyed" report. Surprisingly, we found out later that he never did go there. Perhaps he knew a good tailor.

LOOKING GOOD

Near the end of my career, it was becoming increasingly difficult for coach passengers to get a last-minute First-Class seat on virtually any flight. In fact, it was not at all uncommon to see a computerized "upgrade" list of 60-70 people, all hoping that one of these coveted seats might be theirs. High on the list were elite frequent-flyers and/or elite million-milers. And at the very top were folks who were *both*, and who also had spent actual dollars for their full-fare ticket, rather than using a promo fare or voucher. The top-tiered standbys for First-Class kept an eagle eye on their place in line, as it was constantly updated on gate house information screens.

Working a busy flight to Atlanta one day, I was approached by a well-dressed businesswoman. She smiled pleasantly as she came up to me, then said, "Delta, I have a question. I'm Ruth Beck. For *two weeks* I've been number one on the upgrade list. I'm a trillion-miler, have attained the highest level of Frequent Flyer status that Delta offers and paid a lot of money for my full-fare ticket. Suddenly, though, just an hour ago, I slipped to number two on that list. How could this have happened? I'm not angry, but I just don't see how anyone could have been more qualified or entitled than me"

I told Ms. Beck that I'd look into it. After a few minutes, I had the answer. The new number one on the list was named

Patricia Strong. Indeed, she too, had flown a trillion miles, was at the highest level of frequent flyer and had paid a lot of money for her full-fare ticket. The only difference was, she had paid for it with a *Black American Express Card.* It turned out that Ms. Strong was the only person who got an upgrade for that flight.

I had the chance to do a little more research and read, online, that a Black American Express card was "only offered to the wealthier people in the world."

So, Patricia Strong was one of the wealthiest people in the world. I conveyed all of this information to Ruth Beck and suggested, "Why don't you hold off on boarding a bit, Ms. Beck. Let's see what she looks like."

So, the coach-riding businesswoman and I waited surreptitiously for Ms. Strong to go onto the plane. I clued in the boarding agent about what we were doing. When scanning Strong's First-Class boarding pass, the agent would pause for just a moment and make brief eye contact with me at the desk. Then we'd all know who it was!

I was expecting someone a bit older, dressed in expensive clothes with perfect hair and makeup, wearing diamond earrings, pricey bracelets, top of the line shoes and perhaps carrying a Gucci type bag.

Then Patricia Strong appeared at the boarding door. She was barely out of college! And she was wearing classic jeans and a sweater, with no flashy jewelry, no perfect hair, in basic gym shoes and with very little makeup. She was also carrying a backpack rather than a Gucci bag.

The businesswoman and I looked at each other with great surprise...and then we both laughed. I think that each of us felt a little guilty about the stereotypical "rich lady" we had been expecting. Ms. Strong certainly didn't look like one of the wealthiest people in the world. And that, for us, was a totally *inexpensive* breath of fresh air.

POEM 6 (2003)

The sleek Delta aircraft pulled into the gate,
It was right on time of course.
The journey was smooth, the service was great,
Folks quickly deplaned en force.
A Christmas Eve flight, the people wore smiles,
Attired in green and in red.
Some of them still had to travel for miles,
Before they'd be nestled in bed.

Two from this plane were returning G.I.s,
Now home from the war in Iraq,
Whose parents were waiting with tears in their eyes:
Their sons had safely come back.
Others awaited this same Delta flight,
Each with a warmth in their heart.
Friends and colleagues were waiting that night,
And lovers kept too long apart.

Though countless arrivals come down from the sky
Some hold exceptional pleasure.
Like the days and the months which oft pass us by,
Till Christmas, that time we all treasure
A magical season, with new-fallen snow,
Cookies and presents, and tinsel on trees,
Which makes life, for a while, a big "ho ho ho"
While still thankful upon bended knees.

An airplane arrives, as Christmastime comes,
Each an expected event:
And either to airports or caroler's drums,
Both can seem heaven sent.
Whether waiting for aircraft and who they might carry,
Or waiting for Christmas's joys,
I hope these arrivals make your life merry,
With love and kisses and toys!

And to all whom I know and to all whom I love,
May this yuletime bring warmth to your lives,
With smiles as those planes return from above,
And a promising new year arrives.

FROZEN BRIDGE

On an icy, cold winter night, I met a flight arriving from Miami. It was a late flight, only about half full, and as I slowly moved the jet bridge towards door 1A of the big 767, (adjoining First-Class), I could already see through the airplane's windows that several passengers were moving forward towards that door, grabbing their coats and carry-on bags and bunching up in the front.

Then the jetway stopped. But It was still yards away from the door! No amount of button-pushing or re-setting worked; other than the lights, it was completely dead. As late as it was, there were no mechanics on duty. Via radio, I was in communication with Delta's local operations center, and there the decision was made to have an outdoor, mobile-stair unit connect to the door of the plane. All the passengers would have to deplane down the stairs and across the frozen tarmac to the gatehouse itself. This would be awkward but seemed to be a decent workaround. However, the mobile-stair unit could only be attached to the REAR door of the plane. This was conveyed to the pilots, who, in turn, made an on-board announcement. Therefore, all of the passengers did an about-face and immediately began making their way to the *back* of the plane. The First-Class passengers would now be the last ones off.

The mobile-stair unit was self-propelled. But, in the freezing cold temperatures, it wouldn't start! By now, almost a half hour had passed since the plane had stopped at the gate. No amount of effort could get that stair-machine working. Now what?

Finally, someone came up with another idea: one of the ramp tugs would slowly bump up against the dead jet bridge and actually push it into place on the plane. *Against door 1A.*

Thus, the pilots made another onboard announcement, resulting in the passengers doing *another* about-face and reclaiming their positions in the front of the plane.

When all was said and done, and the jet bridge slowly connected to the plane, I opened the door at 1A. Then, I recall that the passengers practically *sprinted* out but not without hurling a few, choice expletives my way. Who could blame them?

Airplane Etymology 9

A compass *is among the various gauges in the cockpit of a modern airplane. However, the etymology of this word dates back to the 14th century and the French/Latin word* "compas" *At that early time the word only referred to a mathematical device that was round, had a point and was used to draw circles. In fact, a compass is still used today by architectural drafters to create perfectly round circles. Over time, though, a compass also came to be used as a directional device, maintaining its round shape with a floating needle replacing the point.*

FAMOUS FEATHERS, FAMOUS FACES

Most public-contact airline employees occasionally interact with celebrities. The longer one works, the greater is the potential of meeting someone like a movie star, politician or sports legend. In my 45-year career, I saw hundreds of famous passengers as they were booked on flights for which I was responsible. With few exceptions, I treated them like any other passenger, thinking that they'd appreciate some privacy, and preserving their chance to get away, if only for a while, from the fans and the paparazzi. The exceptions to this, however, are all part of brief but notable encounters I specifically had with each of them. Here are some that I most remember.

Jesse Owens: Of the three autographs I ever asked for in all the years I worked, one was one from this great man. He wrote, "Jeff, my best to you always." and signed it, "Jesse Owens, '36 Olympics." What a treasure!

Maria Von Trapp: Ms. Von Trapp checked in for her flight to Burlington, Vermont one afternoon. When I saw the name on her ticket, I said, "Maria Von Trapp? Really? *The* Maria Von Trapp?"

She replied, "Oh, yes!" Until that moment, I had truly thought that "*The Sound of Music*" was a made-for-Hollywood movie, and that Maria Von Trapp was a fictitious character. I told her this.

She smiled, and said, "No, I'm very much alive!" and proceeded to the gatehouse, unbeknownst to anyone else there. However, I must admit that I was surprised at her appearance. I was expecting someone who looked like Julie Andrews. Instead, the real Maria Von Trapp looked more like Kate Smith.

Colonel Harland Sanders: I met the original Colonel Sanders several times as he departed on flights from Chicago to Louisville. He was a bit frail, used a cool, decorative cane, always traveled with an attendant and looked *exactly* like the pictures of him on the KFC logos. However, I had always assumed that "Colonel" was a prior *military* title. No. It was, and is, an *honorary* title, given to certain, esteemed gentlemen as a sign of respect.

Cubby: When I was a kid, one of my favorite TV programs was the "Mickey Mouse Club." Two of the members of that club whom I liked the most, were "Cubby" and "Karen," probably because they were the closest to me in age. Cubby was a little kid, too, but he sure could play the drums! As the years went by, I learned that Cubby's last name was "O'Brien" and that, after the original Mickey Mouse Club, he continued his drumming career. He was still amidst that career when he checked in for a flight one day. I showed my gate partner the name, "Cubby O'Brien" on our computer screen.

My partner had no idea who he was and theorized that he must have been quite a Cubs fan. Anyhow, Cubby himself came up to the desk to verify his seat assignment, and I took the opportunity to chat with him a bit. I then asked him two questions. (1) How had professional drumming changed over the past forty years? And (2) Who did he think the greatest drummer of all time was?

He smiled, sat down in the gatehouse, thought for a few minutes, then came back with his answers. First of all, he felt that drumming had significantly changed, years ago, because the *surface* of the drums themselves had changed. Rather than any natural skin, they were now made of a synthetic material which maintained its tone and timber far longer. Therefore, it wasn't necessary for him to spend time tuning the drums between sets or songs. Secondly, his answer for the greatest, most masterful drummer of all time wasn't Keith Moon or Gene Krupa. Cubby O'Brien felt that, without a doubt, it was Buddy Rich.

Luke Appling: In 1982, in major league baseball's "Old Timer's Game," Hall-of-Fame pitcher, Warren Spahn, was pitching to former Chicago White Sox shortstop, Luke Appling. Appling hit an over-the-fence home run. He was 75 years old! A few days later, he was a passenger on a flight I was assigned to work, and I took the opportunity to get his autograph. His improbable homerun, at age 75, remains one of baseball's most unlikely surprises. Back then, I found it inspiring. I still do.

Challenger: "Challenger" was not a boxing-industry prize fighter, but a large and beautiful bald eagle. He was the live embodiment of the United States symbolic National Bird, and, along with a spectacular cage and personal handler, flew all across America for special patriotic appearances.

They were heading to Salt Lake City and would be a part of the Winter Olympics held that year. His handler had purchased two seats in First-Class. One of them was for the emblematic eagle, whose cage could be attached to the seatbelt. Both of them were allowed to preboard. Perhaps it was my imagination, but I felt that Challenger was looking strong and proud, as well he should be.

Ted Williams: He was the last Major League baseball player to end the season with a .400 batting average, and all of the guys I worked with were so excited to see this famous athlete. Mr. Williams had several fans who followed him down to the gatehouse, and he never hesitated to sign an autograph. One of my Delta colleagues was an amateur baseball player. He had no hesitation about approaching Ted Williams and asking him for some batting advice. At the time, we were using 12-inch, heavy plastic pneumatic tubes to send documents back and forth to our auditing office. Seeing one of those tubes, Williams asked for it. He then told my ball-playing colleague to grasp the end of it, just like it was a bat. After doing so, Ted

Williams suggested a change in the way that my friend's fingers were encircling the handle. For me, it was so cool to see this Hall-of-Famer take the time and patience to give an impromptu batting lesson right in my gatehouse.

Peabody Ducks: Ducks? As in *birds*? Yes, indeed. I remember two or three times when several of the famous Peabody Ducks flew on Delta from Chicago to Memphis. The venerable Peabody Hotel is where they made their well-known morning and evening "performances," strutting along a long, red carpet to greet and end each business day. As I recall, there were two birds to each handler, and these privileged ducks were kept inside beautiful, gilded cages that could be strapped into seats on the plane, much like a child's car seat. Just once at O'Hare, though, I watched as the handlers briefly *let them out* in the gatehouse of the Memphis flight. There, they proceeded to regally walk along a shorter red carpet, right back into their cages. There was not a single ruffled feather as the crowd clapped and cheered!

THE FALLEN

In the past, often there were four different gatehouse employees who might be working a busy flight all at the same time. Such was the case one afternoon when I, as the primary agent, worked next to Marcie, the secondary agent. In addition, we had a third person scheduled to be at the boarding door. His job was to collect tickets and boarding passes from passengers as they went onto the aircraft. Finally, for these hectic flights, there was also one other agent assigned to be a "runner." He would take the collected tickets and boarding passes from the agent at the door and bring them to us at the desk so they could be counted and processed in the computer. Then he would hustle back to the boarding door to get more. Today's runner was named Alberto. He was charming, calm, capable and very fit. He also had eyes that noticeably flashed on those rare instances when he was upset.

On this particular and forever-memorable occasion, Marcie had brought her purse to the gate desk area. It was a very large purse similar to a carpet bag, with two big, floppy handles. Marcie placed the purse securely between us in a little, floor-level, cubbyhole and we went to work, greeting passengers and engaging in the usual, intense activities involved with working the flight. Soon enough it was boarding time.

The third agent went to the gate door, and Alberto started bringing the tickets and boarding passes back to us.

Somehow, as we were working, Marcie's purse fell over. Its two large handles now lay inches off the floor, right next to each other.

We didn't notice.

Then the most unlikely event occurred. On one of his hurried trips back to the boarding door from our desk, Alberto inadvertently placed his right foot directly inside the loop of one of the purse's handles. And then he placed his left foot in the other loop. At that moment, with his momentum carrying him forward, he was hog tied, and down he went like a sack of potatoes. I will never forget that sight as long as I live. As poor Alberto flipped over on his back in the middle of the gate house with his ankles still pinioned by the purse, he looked like an upside-down crab. And then he began kicking and kicking until one foot was free. At that point he was able to *fling* the second purse off the remaining foot. People in the gate house gasped.

Red-faced and embarrassed, Alberto picked himself up, unhurt. He brushed off his clothes, then directed a scathing glance in the direction of Marcie and me at the desk. Talk about flashing eyes! We both had the good sense not to burst out laughing, or I might not be writing this story today

HEADSET HERO

A common accessory for a cell phone is an over-the-ear, hands-free, headset. They look like an oversized hearing aid and can cost hundreds of dollars. One afternoon, a flight came into O'Hare from Atlanta, and passengers started deplaning. Suddenly, one of the flight attendants from the plane ran out to me at the gate desk. In her hand was one of those pricey headsets. "Quick!" she said, "The guy who left this was in First-Class, seat 3A. Page him in the terminal so he can return and get it. Hurry!"

With a few clicks on the computer, I discovered that the man in seat 3A was a Robert Barry. Accessing the airport P.A. system, I immediately paged, "Mr. Robert Barry, please return to Delta's gate E15 to claim a lost article."

No one came, even after I made the same page two more times. Maybe Mr. Barry had already left the terminal, or perhaps he just didn't hear my announcements.

I decided to bring the headset to the baggage service office, along with a copy of his reservation data. Knowing it was an expensive item, I carefully placed it in a convenient and obvious area of the gate desk, knowing that I'd take it with me to the baggage office within a few hours, right after I was done working.

I completely forgot it.

The next day, I was assigned to the same gate, E15 and, to my horror and pure gratitude, there was the headset, exactly where I had left it. Unbelievable. It had been there for hours and hours, even overnight. Furthermore, when I looked at it again, and closely examined Mr. Barry's reservation data, I discovered that he was booked to go back to Atlanta, again in First-Class, seat 3A, *on the very flight I was now working.* Most of the First-Class cabin had already boarded by the time I realized this. I stepped away from the desk for a moment, went on board the plane and approached seat 3A. "Mr. Barry?" I asked.

"Yes?" he replied.

I then took the lost headset from my hand and gave it to him.

"Oh my God!" he exclaimed. "Thank you, thank you, thank you. This is just wonderful! And *this* is why I fly Delta: Service that is *way* above and beyond!"

I simply told him that I was only doing my job (not mentioning the fact that I had completely forgotten his headset, the day before.) That's when Mr. Barry told me he was a personal friend of a Delta Vice President and that he intended to write a letter to him about my "outstanding performance"

Mr. Barry was true to his word and actually wrote to a Delta V.P. Furthermore, a few weeks later, that same Delta V.P. *reprinted the letter in a company-wide publication,* specifically praising "Jeff's extraordinary efforts" in getting this headset back to a grateful passenger. I felt pretty uncomfortable as many of my peers and supervisors complimented me about that letter. Little did they know the whole story.

Note: This last poem is the only one that doesn't take place <u>in</u> an airport, but rather after the airport was left behind. Nevertheless, it reflects my sentiments as a new retiree.

POEM 7 (2015)

I'm at thirty thousand feet as I write this Christmas poem,
Seven thousand miles from family, friends and home.
I leave behind America, the land of milk and honey,
Heading toward a country where folks don't have much money.

In just a few hours' time, the world below has changed,
From mansions and plush condos, so carefully arranged,
To thatch-roofed huts and flimsy shacks along a muddy ditch.
It's such a vivid contrast from the excess of the rich.

I'm happily retired now, with time to contemplate
The blessings I've enjoyed: peace and love and friendships great.
And as I soar on silver wings across the winter sky,
I so appreciate these things that money just can't buy

The country that I'm flying to has poverty replete,
Yet that doesn't dim the smiles of the people on the street.
For Christmas has no borders, no barriers of wealth,
And brings comfort to the ailing, as well as those in health.

There's no need for Yuletide gifts to even be a "thing"
An act of kindness often trumps a shiny golden ring.
Those who live in poverty still seem to find a way
To celebrate the magic that comes on Christmas Day

It may be just across the town, or in a distant land,
But somewhere there is someone who could really use a hand.
Reached by speeding train or plane, or even with your car,
The poor, the sick, the lonely…they don't always live afar.

So, as the month, December, approaches with its zest,
Why not add a thoughtful deed, as you celebrate this fest?
Share this season's warmth and share this season's joy
And watch the smiles appear on a grateful girl or boy!

And as January enters, here's wishing that it's great.
With a whole year full of blessings just waiting on your plate.
And whether you are close to home or are flying far above,
Merry Christmas, everyone! May your lives be full of love.

HEADS UP

For as long as commercial aviation has existed, there have always been passengers who fly or *try* to fly while inebriated. Far too often, folks who were a little under the weather while on the ground, have turned into raging tyrants once their flight has taken off. At cruising altitude, there is a lower level of oxygen in the air of a passenger plane, and this can truly exacerbate an already tipsy condition. For this reason, airline agents have every right to refuse passage to anyone who appears intoxicated or under the influence. Telling someone that they can't fly because they appear to be intoxicated, can be a really challenging situation. Most incidents progress easily with the passenger readily agreeing to go on another flight, after they sober up. But there are also much more stressful, and even scary, occasions when the situation becomes violent.

In my 45-year career as a front-line gate agent and gate PSA for Delta, I dealt with dozens of drunken passengers, primarily before the implantation of TSA security procedures. After 9/11, that number, fortunately, seemed to lessen with each passing year.

However, there were several unique situations involving inebriated passengers that I will always remember. There once was a man who missed his flight, staggering drunkenly into the gate house just to see the plane taxiing away. He screamed for me to get it back. Of course, I refused, whereupon he put both hands around my neck, started squeezing, and asked me if I wanted to die! When I gasped, "No!" he released his hold and walked to the windows of the gate while I called the police.

In another incident, a lady who was obviously under the weather wanted to take her *leashed poodle* into the Delta Crown Room. Upon my polite denial, she slugged me in the stomach.

Another event I clearly recall involved the best man seeing off a departing bride and groom. He was totally blitzed and, for some crazy reason, thought it would be fun to *spritz* me with his girlfriend's perfume. I smelled like sweet gardenia all day and endured many strange looks from both colleagues and customers.

Yet none of the incidents above come close to comparing with something that happened one memorable afternoon between a large, drunken passenger and me. His name was John Malek. He was scheduled to take an early afternoon flight to Little Rock, Arkansas. When he checked in with the gate agent though, his speech was slurred, and he was having difficulty walking. As a PSA on that occasion, I would be responsible for any decision regarding Mr. Malek. Knowing this, the gate agent immediately contacted me. In arriving at the gate, I personally observed Malek for several minutes. He looked and acted quite inebriated and was, without a doubt, in no condition to fly.

Therefore, I approached him and asked if I might see his ticket, then suggested that we talk a bit. For privacy, we went over to a secluded area of the gate house, out of view of the public, and I sat down next to him. "Mr. Malek," I said, "I think you've had a little too much to drink, and we need to book you on the next flight to Little Rock." John Malek didn't seem to understand. So, I repeated, more assertively, "You'll be taking the *next* flight to Little Rock, sir, assuming you get some coffee and are back to normal by then"

At this, Malek did something so unexpected, so unbelievable, that I cringe when I think about it, even now. Suddenly, he leaped from his seat, stood directly in front of me, and, with his left hand, grabbed me by my hair! *My hair! OW!*

In all of the Delta Passenger Service manuals I ever read, there was nothing in them that suggested what to do when a drunken passenger was painfully pulling your hair.

I politely asked Mr. Malek, "Please let go of my hair." No response. Then I softly placed my own right hand next to his hair-grabbing left hand and in this manner, tried to gently release it from my hair. No luck. As my pain worsened, and his grip got tighter and tighter, I only had one other alternative. Brute force. Using a lot more strength, I *forcibly slammed* my right hand into his left hand. I expected that his grip would instantly release with my powerful blow. It did not! Instead, he ended up *ripping a chunk of hair right off of my poor scalp.*

Then he reached back with his huge right hand and said words which made me quiver, "I've got a notion to *pop* you one!"

What could I do? Desperate, I suddenly exclaimed, "Wait! Look at what your ticket says here!" This distracted him! He let go of my hair and peered at the ticket I was holding, allowing me to scramble away to safety in a more public area of the gate. Eventually, I was able to withstand the sharp headache from my lost locks and call the police who dragged him away in handcuffs. For days afterward, I had a large, noticeable bald spot. Also, I learned, painfully, to always have plenty of people around before confronting someone who was under the influence. It truly was a hair-raising experience.

LIGHTS OUT

As the big L1011 from Atlanta was making its final approach towards O'Hare, the pilot radioed ahead to say that they "needed maintenance" upon arrival. These two words always elicited worry and stress to those of us on the ground, since that inbound plane was normally scheduled to turn right around and leave again. In this particular instance, our mechanics at O'Hare already knew that the problem was a broken light under the wing. However, it was a huge, hefty bulb and replacing it would take some time.

Compounding the situation was the fact that our maintenance facility did not stock that particular underwing light. However, we could purchase one from another O'Hare airline. This was quite a common practice. It just would take a little longer.

Since I was working the outbound flight back to Atlanta, I needed to let the passengers know about any potential delay. I conveyed this information to the passengers via the P.A. and told them to expect a 40-minute delay, though the pilot felt confident that some of that time could be reduced en route. Thus, the many travelers who were changing planes in Atlanta would still be able to make their connecting flights.

As time went on, I continued to make occasional and reassuring gatehouse updates. Eventually, I was advised that the mechanics were on their way with the new lamp.

Finally, I could actually see the maintenance vehicle approaching our plane on the ramp. "Folks," I said, "If you look out the gatehouse windows *right now*, you will actually be able to witness our highly-trained mechanics installing the new light."

Dozens of passengers rushed to the windows and peered out. Even from my position at the gate desk, I could also watch exactly what was happening on the ramp below.

At last, the new lamp arrived planeside. Since the distance was great from the tarmac to under the wing, one of the mechanics got into a personal lifting device, carefully cradling the bulb. Slowly, he was elevated into the proper position, ready for the installation itself. Half the gatehouse was now looking out the window. Carefully, the mechanic lifted the heavy lamp into precisely the right position, completely unaware of all the anxious eyes that were watching from the windows.

But then, suddenly, he fumbled his precious cargo. It dropped out of his highly trained hands and fell to the ground, breaking into a hundred pieces!

There was a brief moment of silence and shock. And then the cries of, "Oh, no!" and "Aw, Spit!" and "*Now* what's going to happen?" erupted from all who had been following my happy announcements, watching the proceedings. Many of them were customers who were hoping to make their connecting flights, as I had once felt so positively about. Now, dozens needed to be rebooked. In some instances, the arrival at their final destination would be hours later.

Ultimately, another replacement light arrived on the scene. This time, I didn't say one word. Under the recent circumstances, it just wouldn't have been a very bright idea.

EXPLOSIVE DEVICE

As Flight 820 pulled into the gate at O'Hare, little did I know that I was about to become involved in one of the most memorable incidents in my entire career. Wearing my red PSA jacket, I was, as usual, meeting and greeting all the deplaning passengers as they exited the jetway and made their way onto the concourse. However, after only a dozen or so passengers deplaned, there were no more in sight. I assumed someone was temporarily delaying the line, perhaps retrieving an overhead bag.

However, after several moments a flight attendant came out, looking scared and shaken. She came up to me and said, "There is a man on board who says he is carrying a bomb in his bag and that he is taking hostages. All of the other passengers are afraid to move"

Quickly, I grabbed the airline radio I was carrying and, contacting all of the Delta departments at the airport, said, "Attention, attention, attention, we have a situation involving a potential bomb and hostages on inbound flight 820. Contact airport security immediately"

Then I entered the jetway towards the plane and towards whatever was waiting on board. To my surprise, one of the pilots was talking to an angry looking man, just beyond the door of the aircraft. The man was carrying a small bag. On the plane, remaining passengers were lined up, still waiting to depart.

The pilot turned to me (we knew each other) and said, "Jeff, this is Mr. Kassi. He's very upset. I was just…"

Kassi looked at the pilot, looked back at the lined-up passengers, and turned to me, saying loudly, "I will talk to no one except *you*!"

Oh my God! Now I was the only person who could speak to an angry man who claimed to be carrying a bomb.

I asked Mr. Kassi if perhaps we could walk out into the hall together. I had a microphone from the radio in my ear and on it I heard someone say, "Get his bag tag stubs." So, as we walked, I asked him for his ticket envelope. Sure enough, stapled inside were two bag stubs. I secretly removed them, palmed them, then dropped them behind us as we made our way to the gatehouse. Kassi stumbled several times as we walked and was yelling incoherently, but never letting go of the bag he was clutching. My Delta colleagues quickly retrieved the bag stubs and matched them with two suitcases in the hold of the plane. Those two suitcases were then taken to a remote area of the airport, possibly to be opened by trained bomb-squad experts.

Meanwhile, Mr. Kassi and I walked off the jetway, going across the concourse to an empty gatehouse, where I suggested that we sit and talk. By this time, Chicago police were on the scene but stayed well away from the two of us.

I turned to Kassi and said, "You are scaring a lot of people with your behavior. Why are you so upset?"

Kassi's speech was slurred, and there was a definite smell of alcohol on his breath when he yelled, "They wouldn't get out of my way!"

"So, you told them you were carrying a bomb in that bag?"

"Yes!" he replied. "And now I will show you what is in this bag!"

My heart stopped as he opened the bag.

Inside was a toy truck with a package of batteries.

It took me a minute to start breathing again. I gave the all-clear sign to the police and airport security officials who now were everywhere. One of them approached me and asked if I thought Kassi was simply an intoxicated and possibly deranged individual, or someone who had posed a serious threat to the flight and its crew? I replied that I felt confident that he was nothing more than a crazy drunk. I later learned that the police took him away to a local cell, rather than to federal prison where he could have faced charges of aircraft terrorism.

Looking back at this incident now, I realize that during the time I was with Mr. Kassi, I was fairly calm and collected, except for that brief, heart-stopping moment when he opened the bag. Immediately afterwards, though, my heart rate skyrocketed, and I shook with relief. Finally, as I am writing these very words and recalling all of the violent bombings that have occurred since flight 820 arrived that day, I'm filled with the thoughts of what *could* have happened. I was lucky. We all were.

HEAT STROKE
(This additional story, did not actually happen AT the airport.)

It was about 10:30 pm one chilly evening, as I drove away from O'Hare after a busy day at work. Little did I realize then that this trip home would be forever burned into my mind.

Despite the coolness of the night, I noticed that the dashboard temperature dial in my car indicated that it was starting to overheat a bit. I was driving a Jeep Cherokee which was in fine running condition, and, in fact, I'd just had the oil changed and the engine tuned up the day before. Nevertheless, the farther along I drove, the higher the temperature gauge climbed. Initially, I wasn't sure I'd make it all the way home. I kept glancing at the gauge, hoping to see that inexorable temperature rise start to diminish. No luck. The arrow in the dial had now crept up to the "Alert! Danger!" mark, but, since I was now so very close to home, I kept on driving. I knew I could make it.

By the time I pulled into our driveway, the needle was jammed *above* the danger mark. But I was home. Whew! It was now 11:30 pm. I decided to leave the car out of the garage to cool down faster.

As I left the car and walked towards my front door, I glanced back at the cooling vehicle. Suddenly, I noticed a *flicker of flame* below it! This was unnerving, to say the least.

However, since my car was parked really close to both my house and garage, and all I could think of was that, if it burst into flames, those structures would catch on fire too.

So, I hustled back into the car, started it up and drove it to the end of the driveway. Just this simple movement made those flickering flames disappear and I was relieved. Leaving the Jeep again, I walked the length of the driveway and returned to the front door of the house. Then, I turned one last time to look at the car...and saw, to my horror, that the flames had returned!

I realized then that the act of driving the car was creating enough wind that it kept the fire at bay. So, I ran back and started driving again. I knew that, when I stopped, the car would ignite once more.

I drove to the fire department.

Leaving the car, I raced inside and yelled at the desk sergeant, "Quick! My car is right in front of the station, and it's about to burst into flames. Quick!"

The fire sergeant looked at me as if I were inebriated or crazy. But then he looked out at the car. Sure enough, little flames soon appeared below the chassis. He pushed a button and somewhere an alarm sounded, and within seconds two local fireman appeared from inside the station. They both grabbed foam-type extinguishers and proceeded to whoosh flame retardant and foam onto the undercarriage of my car for several minutes. Then they stopped. All of us held our breaths and waited, while the firemen were ready to spring back into action at the slightest flicker. Nothing.

Fifteen minutes later, the car was completely quiet and surprisingly cool. My home was less than a mile away so I knew I could easily make the trip with no worry that it would overheat again. However, just before I left, one of the firemen came up to me and said, "Mr. Degner, I've been a firefighter for thirty years. But this is the first time in my life that someone has *brought the fire to me!*"

The problem turned out to be that when the professional oil change had happened the day before, the oil reservoir had not been properly closed. Oil had been very slowly dripping out ever since. This is what had initially caused the car to overheat, and, in fact, it was the leaking oil that had been catching fire.

LAUGHTER

One of the constants in my career with Delta was my frequent use of humor. I used it in my interactions with my colleagues, with flight attendants and pilots, and especially with the unsuspecting public. In particular, I became well known for my "unique" gatehouse announcements, which invariably included some comical elements. Why? It made customers pay more attention to the statements that were truly important. It also put smiles on their faces. And it was fun for me, too.

I would page nonexistent celebrities to the desk, make up gross-sounding airborne meals and tell standby passengers that their odds of getting on the flight increased if they had samples of home-made pastries. I'd ask passengers if they wanted to check their children *into the baggage bin* and sometimes, on empty flights, announced that people wearing glasses or wearing hats could board ahead of anyone else.

On occasion, I'd declare that certain rows on the plane were designated as "quiet zone rows," with passengers sitting in those rows required to be silent for the entire flight. At other times, seeing Delta's regular First-Class passengers lining up and preparing to board first, as usual, I would create super-high levels of frequent-flyer-status, like, "Plutonium" or "Titanium" and then invite only these *elite* customers to board. The First-

Class passengers invariably looked shocked. Some even asked what they had to do to become a Plutonium-level flyer.

One day, a man with his ten-year-old son came up to my counter. He said, "Many years ago, I was ten years old myself and traveling with *my* dad on Delta. I don't remember too much about the flight, but I never forgot the crazy announcements the gate agent made. It was you! And now my own son can have the same pleasure. I'm so glad you're still around!"

The celebrities that I'd page to the desk evolved with the times. Early on, I paged "Mother Teresa." Later, during the O.J. Simpson trial, it was "Lance Ito." Still later, it was Dennis Rodman, Hillary Rodham Clinton and Brittany Spears...all names that were believable enough to make passengers look around.

When professional teams of all sorts were booked on a flight I was working, I made it a point to acknowledge their presence to the entire gate house. But whatever their true sport was, from college basketball to international soccer players, and whether they were young or old, male or female, I always introduced them as a famous *synchronized swim team*. The reactions were always priceless.

When "zone" boarding became popular, there were usually four or five different zones. Almost all such boarding was according to letters, like "zone A." The passengers in zone A were always elite frequent flyers or those who were holding seats in the First-Class cabin. Even though the zone A customers were able to enter the plane first, oftentimes they would still line up in front of the boarding door, increasingly anxious, some even appearing impatient, inching closer and closer as time went by.

Seeing this, I would go over the usual pre-boarding instructions, and then (finally!) announce that the first group to board would be those passengers in *Group 1*. What? Group 1? *There was no Group 1!* This invariably caused great surprise and confusion amongst the already-lined-up people who were seated in zone A. That is, until they looked my way and saw the big grin on my face. In addition, though, I'd tell passengers from Wisconsin to board in Zone 17 and Packer fans to take another flight.

I learned how to play personal songs on the gatehouse speakers. Thus, at Christmastime, it was not uncommon to hear "Jingle Bell Rock" or "Grandma Got Run Over by a Reindeer" blasting through the air. Alternatively, a song by Johnny Cash might be heard by all. The smiles were unanimous.

On Halloween and April Fool's Day, I would always bring a small, rubber mouse to work. It was very realistic and never failed to elicit screams of terror from co-workers and flight attendants, even though I did it year after year. At other times, I even used, very cautiously, a bit of humor when dealing with an angry passenger. For example, an irate businessman once came up to me, furious because of a weather-caused delay on his flight to Atlanta. "What's the weather *really* like there?" he demanded. "I just saw on the news that it looks fine!"

I replied that currently in Atlanta there was rain, fog and widespread pestilence. "Pestilence?" he asked. "Did you say *pestilence?*"

"Yep," I replied with the hint of a smile, "pestilence." He shook his head in disbelief, and his anger completely disappeared. Then, with a smile of his own, he left, saying, "That was a good one, Delta"

The newspaper column below appeared in
the Atlanta Journal many years ago.
It is reprinted with permission from the author, Elliott Brack.

Sitting around an airport can be awfully boring, even though your airplane is to depart soon. When there's a delay, or when you have lots of time between flights, it's even more boring. Last week, ready to fly from Chicago to Atlanta, we were sitting and reading before boarding the plane. When a voice from the counter came on the microphone, we started hearing the same old patter you can hear at any gate.

"Good afternoon, ladies and gentlemen, welcome to Delta Flight 1583 to Atlanta. We'll be boarding the plane today by rows in just a short time, according to the Geneva Convention."

That stunned a few around me.

"What did he say?" one wondered, as several of us snapped to the alert. Strangers started addressing one another. "Did he say according to the Geneva Convention? What does that mean?" Maybe it means they're taking prisoners," one said. Another chimed in: "Why not board by Roberts Rules of Order?" Another figured: "Maybe it means women and children should go first."

Soon the Delta agent was telling us that passengers could only take aboard the plane luggage of a certain size, "or else we have scissors and knives and compression devices for those whose luggage is too big."

By now we were all wondering, "Is this guy for real?"

When telling about the meal for us on the plane, the agent announced that passengers would get to enjoy the new Delta Deli service, which they could pick up as they got on the plane. "Today's menu consists of turkey on either pumpernickel or a roll, with anchovies and onion." As we were wondering how many people liked anchovies, the agent came back on, saying, "I'm kidding about the anchovies and onion, though we do have turkey sandwiches."

By then, nearly all of us had caught on that we had in the Delta agent something of a stand-up comic on the mike. Yet there was more. About that time, he asked: "Will passenger Leonardo DiCaprio please report to the counter?" Then, just before passengers started to queue up, the agent told us that "passengers may board ahead of the others if they are traveling with infants, are senior citizens or are from Wisconsin."

His final words mentioned it was time "for passengers holding memberships in platinum, gold, silver or stainless-steel clubs to board."

We eyed his badge and learned that Jeff Degner was the one behind the voice entertaining us. Folks around me seemed to enjoy the diversion away from the usual humdrum announcement. It enlivened our boarding.

When times were really slow, I occasionally created fictitious standby passengers and put them on the standby list for my gate agent colleagues to page to the desk. I used many of the names over and over, yet the same employee might fall into the trap several times, while I watched, listened, and grinned, until they saw me and realized what had happened yet again! Here are some of the names I used, and that were paged out loud: Mr. Ben Dover. Mr. Jim Shuze. Ms. Polly Esther. Manuel Labor. Mrs. Claire Voyant. Paul Bearer. Justin Case. Neil Down. There are lots more, but these were among my favorites and seemed to work every time.

There also was a way that special remarks could be added to a passenger record. They would be noticed in the final, printed paperwork for a flight and were informational comments associated with customers who required wheelchairs, or unaccompanied minors, or folks who might have dietary issues or hearing impairments, etc. They also could identify people who didn't speak English. Once, I discovered that a woman I knew was just about to leave on a flight. In the nick of time, I put some special remarks in her record indicating that (1) She only spoke Danish, and (2) She was carrying a *tiny cat* in her tote bag. Later, I found out that shortly after takeoff, one of the flight attendants came up to her, knelt down in front of her and slowly and quite clearly said, "CAT...IN...BAG? CAT...IN...BAG?" My friend had no idea what she was talking about.

In a similar instance, I found out that a pal of mine, Dusty, was taking one of our flights to Atlanta. In his record, I added that he spoke Russian only. On his way to Atlanta, everything went smoothly. But then, for his flight home, he decided to see if he could get his seat switched to an emergency-exit-row seat. For several minutes, the gate agent in Atlanta tried to get Dusty's request accepted in the computer. No luck. Dusty wondered what was taking so long. Then the agent got a supervisor to help. After a few more minutes, the supervisor looked closely at him and loudly said, *"Do you speak English?"* Somehow, Dusty knew just who the culprit was. The "Russian only" remark in his record prevented any seat assignment in the emergency row.

Finally, there are dozens of flight attendants who declare that they are still seeking revenge for what I did to them. The scenario was always the same. I would rush onto a fully loaded plane just a few minutes before departure. In my hand was a wallet. Indicating the wallet, I would tell the nearest flight attendant that it had been left in the gate house! Fortunately, I had the owner's name on a scrap of paper, and if the attendant could simply *page* that person on board, I could quickly return it. The name on the paper was, "Hugh Jass," and it wasn't until the actual announcement was made – and the airplane was full of laughter – that the realization dawned of just how that name sounded! In fact, there was one time when the flight attendant said she was just too busy to make the page. Hearing this, the captain himself got on the aircraft's P.A. system and, deeply and authoritatively, paged Mr. Jass. I'm on his revenge list, too.

FAREWELL

Clearly, my Delta career had an unbelievable number of unique, challenging, funny and even scary incidents. It also was balanced with my attempts at good humor and fun. I consider myself truly fortunate to have held the same public-contact job with a great airline for 45 years, and to have appreciated each one of those years right up to the very end. How many workers can say that today?

Before closing I want to share a poem written by an airline pilot on his last trip home. The perspective is different, as the author speaks of "a million tracks across the sky," whereas for me, I think back about the million passengers that came my way. But the sentiment he expresses truly mirrors the emotion I was feeling as I dispatched my own last flight and slowly walked back to the gatehouse. Somehow, that jetway seemed especially long that day. I'll never forget how so many of my fellow employees were waiting for me, taking final pictures and applauding. Moments later, I turned in my airline I.D. badge forever. Then I cried like a baby. I was surely ready for retirement and, today, am enjoying it immensely. But saying goodbye to my Delta career was so bittersweet. It still is. Here's that poem:

FINAL APPROACH
(Author Unknown)

Homeward bound and streaking through the vast and midnight sky,
Still free, above the earth, amidst this final flight.
Like diamonds splayed upon a jeweler's cloth,
The brightly shining stars surround this lonely night.

No more do aircraft wires whistle with the wind,
No more goggled men, in leather suits, flying just by feel.
With digital protection and technology's embrace,
We soar like massive birds on wings of tempered steel.

Not so long ago was the roar of many warplanes,
And the sound of distant gunfire. These can still induce a pang,
Of a frightened boy, too soon a man, and far away from home,
Planning yet another strike from high above Da Nang

The wonders of this world are not shackled to the ground,
For here above the clouds, the awe comes shining through:
The dancing fire of summer's storms, a city's sparkling lights,
A golden setting sun as witnessed by a privileged few.

This legacy of soul and flight I now must leave to others,
To see what I have seen and do what I have done.
But the joys of life can sometimes slowly fade away,
And memories become vague, if not shared with anyone.

And now the time draws near, just one last turn for home.
I watch the trusty compass swing, it plays its final part.
Before my eyes, the runway lights lack their usual welcome glow
For they are calling back to land a most reluctant heart.

For one more lasting moment, everything is still,
My mind replaying all those cockpit years I've flown:
With countless faces at my side, we raced beside the wind,
And shared a way of life that earthbound man has never known.

I knew this joy-filled dream would never last forever,
And yes, the time has passed so very swiftly by.
But how fortunate I've been, to create so many contrails,
And etch a million tracks across the endless sky!

Thank you for reading these memoirs! I'm forever grateful to my dear airline friends and colleagues for their support and encouragement over the years. As this manuscript was being created, I also want to acknowledge the enthusiastic proofreading assistance from my wife, Marcie, as well as from my friends, Fotena and Leslie. I benefitted further from the help of my excellent editor, Julie Kendrick, and from Wasteland Press for putting everything together. But most of all, thanks to all of the passengers, in and out of these pages, without whom this book would never have taken off.

I wish you joy, adventure, and on-time departures to wherever your next destination is.

ABOUT THE AUTHOR

Jeff Degner is a free-lance writer whose stories and poems have appeared in a variety of books, newspapers and magazines. With their senior canine, Luna, Jeff and Marcie, make their home in Barrington, Illinois. Both love to travel and during the winter enjoy cheering on their favorite NFL team, though it isn't the same one. Besides writing and dabbling in genealogy, Mr. Degner is an avid pickleball player. He also is the president of the Illinois/Indiana chapter of Healing the Children, (HTC) a volunteer-based, non-profit charity whose purpose is facilitating vital medical assistance for needy children. In fact, proceeds from the sale of this book will be going directly to HTC. Jeff is always waiting to see just whatever life's next adventure is, around the corner or around the world. He can be reached at deltawriter90@gmail.com

Here's a final smile to last a while: Just follow the directions on the back cover!

Made in the USA
Monee, IL
29 October 2021

80617152R00066